Connecting with Nature's Angels

The World of Faeries, Elementals & Nature Spirits

By Blake Cahoon

Twilight Sky Media

Also by Blake Cahoon

Connecting with Celestial Wisdom: The World of Angels & Archangels

Dedicated to Queen Jejaia, King Duke and to all those who believe in magic....

A special thank you to those who helped make this book a reality.

Twilight Sky Media
9903 3rd Avenue
Pleasant Prairie, WI 53158, USA

Connecting with Nature's Angels: The World of Faeries, Elementals & Nature Spirits by Blake Cahoon

PRINTING HISTORY
2nd Edition

For information, address:
Twilight Sky Media
9903 3rd Avenue, Pleasant Prairie, WI 53158
Connect Online: www.TwilightSkyMedia.com

ISBN-13: 978-1505535921
ISBN-10: 1505535921

Printed in the United States of America

Table of Contents

Chapter One:
Exploring the World of the Fey

It is a warm summer night, with the moon half full. You sit in a backyard, sipping cool lemonade, comfy in your lawn chair, near a colorful garden which now is hidden in the shadows. Tiny burst of lights flicker among the shadows creating a magical feeling.

A smile comes to your lips as you watch the fireflies dance in the night as the night stirs your imagination of childhood memories and stories of old, where magical creatures ruled the night and the day.

As a person living in modern times we have to stretch our imagination to see or feel the magic of ordinary fireflies dancing in the moonlight. But to the imagination of English countryside peasants in pre-Christian times these mysterious flickering lights of the night may have inspired the myths and legends of the world of the fairy.

Today we are familiar with the tales of the fairy through the magic of Disney, whose animated world brought us the Blue Fairy of Pinocchio, the fairy godmother of Cinderella, and of course the Peter Pan's companion of Tinkerbelle. Today's children are well exposed to fairy tales through TV and movies, video games and books.

Today's depiction of fairies is of small magical beings with wings and even a fairy wand. They live in nature, among the flowers of the field and in the woods. We think of fairies as good people who grant wishes and help humans. As children we love the feeling that the idea of a fairy world gives us – an enchanted world where any possibility might happen.

But unlike Peter Pan, we have to grow up and the childhood fantasy world of fairies, elves, brownies and trolls disappear as our childhood disappears. We are taught that the world of magic doesn't exist and possibilities are for dreamers. Most of us do grow up; but for the creative soul possibilities remain real and dreams can come true. And fairies—well, they may exist after all, beyond the world of our simple imagination.

Are you a creative soul?

This book is for creative and inspired souls – who can look beyond what is taught as "real" and may accept something a bit more fanciful. What we've been taught about the myths and legends of fairies may have just been the start of a deeper, more exciting adventure. Are you an explorer?

According to legends and mythology, the world of the fairy has its roots in pre-Christian times. We tend to think of the fairy world as coming out of Great Britain, but tales of tiny beings with worlds of their own have global reach.

All across our world, stretching back eons are tales of magical, often misunderstood or mischievous beings who live half in the shadows and half in our world. Stories became more prominent during medieval times when storytellers began sharing their tales of this mysterious fairy world and artists began to bring those stories to life with pictures.

But think of the possibilities: could a part of these stories be true? Could a tale of fancy be rooted in reality?

What if there was another world beyond the one we know? Where nature spirits were real? Where the world of the fairy wasn't just make-believe? Where the energy of nature mingled with the animal kingdom and provided a world we simply can't see with our own five senses?

Can you believe?

When you start to research the original stories of fairies – you'll see that it was man's early fears that created worlds of unseen creatures to explain the world of night and day. Early man created tales to ease the fears of the noises in the night, the mysteries of the weather, of the sea and of the woods.

Superstition ran high and there were ways to appease the unseen forces, with rites and rituals. These unseen forces turned into gods and often demons – good guys and bad guys. Obviously one wanted the good guys on your side and to keep the bad guys away. Various stories were told of both sides and various rituals and rites kept the good guys on your side and the bad guys far away as possible.

The world of the fairies emerged from their stories and to early man and woman, this world was as real as our own is today. They believed. So the stories, myths and legends grew with time.

Today we think of this as fancy tales – fairy tales. But early man believed and even today the legends seem to sway belief in this world. Ask someone from Ireland if they believe in leprechauns or someone from England if they believe in fairies – and you might be surprised that the belief still exists in many areas – especially in the countryside. They still believe.

In the United States, we don't have a tendency to believe in fairies. We're okay with ghosts and angels. But beyond these two categories of the unseen world, we're pretty closed minded.

Although some of that is changing as we enter a 'new age' of enlightenment into the invisible world of energy, creatures and beings. In late 2011, an Associated Press poll said that 8 out of 10 Americans believed in angels. While most people were in the Christian religion category there were others which didn't have a religious preference who also believed in angels.

Would it surprise you to learn that fairies are categorized under the wider banner of angels? This idea was first launched by medieval writers and scholars, and has been carried forward to today's definition of fairies and angels. Fairies have been called nature's angels since they are part of the angelic realm.

Thus we have the title for this book about fairies –except our journey and look into this magical realm is from the perspective of the creative and inspired soul –from those who believe. Still. Today.

For once you begin to believe in one aspect of the angelic realm, your journey will take you to wider horizons of discovery. I know my journey did. And while at first I didn't believe—I now do. I'll tell you how I arrived at this conclusion soon, in an upcoming chapter.

But first I have to tell you that as a child, I 'knew things'. Things that others didn't see; didn't know or could not grasp. My father instilled in me a sense of curiosity and wonder; my mother was much more logical. Somewhere in between people said I had a great imagination, at a very early age.

We lived on a small estate, once farmland. Part of the estate had a house that held ghosts –which I wasn't scared of and somewhere along the line I found I could communicate with.

Growing up my fascination of things paranormal, spooky and metaphysical grew. I studied and grew in my knowledge and in my abilities. Regular communication with the dead was commonplace and in my adult years I began expanding my abilities of conversations with more advanced souls –spirit guides and angels. It was a hop, skip and a jump to communicate with the world of nature's angels. Yet their world was much different than the others. I was compelled to tell their story as I grew to know them; the accumulation of that knowledge resulting in the writing of this book.

Do you believe?

I know I didn't until one day….I did. Would you like to come on a magical journey of discovery into a world unlike any other? Then please do….leave your doubts at the door….and venture into the world of the fey.

The spelling of the word – faeries vs. fairies

I found something out during the course of writing and editing this book: there are two ways of spelling the subject of this book: fairy or faery.

While I began this book using the term "fairy", I have since learned that the term fairy is used by those who strictly believe that these divine beings are a fairy-tale and nothing more. Those who believe or want to believe, use the more ancient version of the word: faery or faeries.

Therefore, as this book is about faeries, not fairies, I have changed the term throughout from this point forward. For the person who wants to believe: call them faeries, not fairies—and prove to them that you do believe!

Chapter Two:
My Introduction to the Faeries

As a child, there were several special television programs my sister and I looked forward to each year. These programs were shown only once per year, if that, and each time they aired on network TV, it was a special event.

There was no cable or satellite TV back when I was child. Nor were there videotapes or DVDs, so we couldn't watch certain programs at any time or day. We only had 3 channels to choose from in those days. These channels were the three big networks: ABC, CBS and NBC.

So in order to see these beloved programs, we had to wait patiently until they aired again. We eagerly waited for these special TV events and had our own special rituals that included popcorn and staying up late, when each program finally was shown.

Those programs were "Wizard of Oz" with Judy Garland as Dorothy, "Rodgers & Hammerstein's' Cinderella" and "Peter Pan"—the Mary Martin as Peter version.

I loved each of these programs – the travel found in "Oz", the romance found in "Cinderella" and for "Peter Pan" the child-like wonder of a magical land that had pirates and faeries. The song "I Won't Grow Up" still resonates with me, as any of my friends will tell you.

And of course there was that special moment in "Peter Pan", where Tinkerbell drinks the poison and the audience had to clap and state that they believe in faeries, so Tinkerbell might be healed and live. And of course, we all clapped at the black and white TV stating that we believed in faeries, eager to bring the tiny ball of mystical light back to life. For she was Peter's favorite friend, next to Wendy, and she helped the children fly with her magical faerie dust. And didn't we all want to fly? Perhaps if she lived then we would learn how to fly too.

I know I wanted to fly; and so I clapped and clapped, and soon Tinkerbell was saved and Peter's adventure continued. And the secret to flying was to think happy thoughts—along with a dash of faerie dust.

We delighted in the wondrous tale of Peter Pan, Wendy and Tinkerbell, year after year. And when I played outside in the yard, I would seek out the faeries among the flowers in the garden or among the tree branches that I often climbed. I believed in the faeries' magical powers. Such is the life of a child.

But unlike Peter Pan—I did grow up. And eventually the question of the belief in faeries was tossed to the back of the closet along with childish toys, like stuffed animals and baby dolls.

Of course during my childhood and into my adult years, I did find that I believed in some aspects of an unseen world, for I believed in ghosts. My adventures with ghosts went beyond fairytales—I received quite positive proof that they existed. Eventually my beliefs expanded into the world of spirit guides and angels. I found I believed in them, as more experiences with this realm came into being during my adult years.

But while some of my contemporaries still believed in the world of faeries and other magical beings, I began to question: did I really believe that faeries actually existed? Perhaps as a child I might have; but as an adult? No, I finally decided; they were part of a mythical land of other enchanting creatures such as leprechauns, elves, brownies, mermaids and unicorns. Right?

I had even done some research on these fictional creatures when I wrote a short story for a DAW anthology about elves. Elves are part of the faerie realm, along with brownies, sprites and leprechauns, according to the literature I researched. But all were mythical beings.

No, I'm afraid I didn't believe in faeries...until one day....well something weirder than normal happened.

I believe it was a dreary weekend day, in the late afternoon, sometime in the late 1990's. I was lying in bed, reading a book about angels and spirit guides. This book was great I thought, as I lay there in my Oak Park apartment. It had lots of neat information about angels and spirit guides that confirmed so much of what I already had learned from both my guides and from my angels, who I just begun to accept as real.

Now before I go on, I must back up and tell you that this apartment was in an old building, built in the early 1900's. The electricity, heating and plumbing were updated probably in the 1950's or 1960's. There was only one circuit in that small bedroom and so if there were an interruption in the electricity, all the lights would flicker at once.

In my bedroom that dreary afternoon, were two lamps on my headboard, illuminating the room. Across the room was my stereo unit, which I usually switched to my CD player, as opposed to the radio. The volume had been left at a normal range the last time it was on.

I had two cats at the time: Selena and Sammy. As I was engrossed in my book, I wasn't paying much attention to where either of them was specifically, although they usually hung out near me. I really was enjoying this book.

I was almost at the end of the book…in fact I was now turning to the last chapter and I turned the page of the book to see that the last chapter was about—faeries! What!!??

I groaned and was so disappointed! This book had given me so much insight about angels and spirit guides – both of which really I believed in. But faeries!? They were make-believe!! They weren't real!!! Why were they in this book?! I lamented this discovery out loud for about thirty seconds or more, when suddenly I started to hear something rustling in the corner by the stereo.

I frowned and started reading the last dang chapter which began describing faeries and treating them as real beings. Just as the angels and spirit guides were real beings. This last chapter was invalidating everything else I had read in the book, as far as I was concerned! I grumbled, only vaguely aware of the rustling in the corner.

I was frustrated and disappointed, yet I kept reading, grumbling all along and wanting to quit the book there and then, willing to throw away all I had learned up to that point and was just beginning to believe in.

The rustling sound was getting louder. It sounded as if one of the cats were playing with a cat toy; it sounded like cellophane crumbling. And it was getting louder by the minute.

I finally looked over at the corner where the noise was coming from, where I was sure I'd find a cat playing. "Sam! Selena!" I said in an un-necessarily harsh tone as I sat up and looked over, already frustrated by the book's content, and now by the interruption.

But both cats were asleep at the foot of my bed. "What the…?" I mumbled and saw nothing in the corner to make such a loud racket. The heat wasn't on and I knew that I had no mice or bugs in the apartment – the cats would have stopped them long ago. The noise subsided immediately.

Frowning, I settled back down determined to read again, despite the subject matter. The book continued on about elementals – nature's kinfolk and how they could help us and talk with us. Again I felt my wave of disbelief wash over me and I was about to give up on the book completely, when suddenly the stereo popped on. I heard it pop and looked over to see that the audiometer was displaying sound, yet there was no sound coming out of the speakers. The radio was on and the volume was turned down to zero. "What the—" I thought.

I immediately noted that the stereo had come on without benefit of flicking the electric lights by my head. I put the book down and rolled out of bed to investigate. The cats glanced up briefly but were too sleepy to pay much attention to what was becoming more obvious to me.

I played with the stereo for a minute and noted there wasn't any reason for the weird sound – unless…. Then I smiled shyly, as one of my spirit guides came to me and whispered, "For someone in your business, you're awfully quick to judge what is real and what is not."

I let out a deep sigh, relenting the fact that I had just been had. "Okay, I get the message – you are real," I said out loud to the room. There was almost a slight breeze that went through the room at that moment and a sense of settling in my soul. These were the faeries – making themselves known to me for the first time. They needed me to believe in them – for so many reasons, which I would find out later.

They had caused the rustling noise and the stereo to come on mysteriously.

That was the day I acknowledged the existence of faeries. I went back to my book and began to re-read what I had read and continued to read with renewed interest and a fresh perspective.

My lesson on belief and disbelief was in full force that day. I can admit when I'm wrong and that day—I was wrong. Faeries really did exist.

Since that day I have learned more and have actually seen the tiny creatures called nature's angels. That day was my first encounter. Since then, I have been lead to learn more and to teach others about these wonderful yet mysterious beings. For me, I know my journey with the faerie realm had just begun.

Chapter Three:
A History of Faeries

The origin of the belief in faeries can be traced back to the early Celtic peoples of what is now Great Britain, or as far back as the Greeks. Mythical creatures such as Pan of Greek mythology are part of early man's exploration of a world that today seems like a fantasy.

But to early man, such fantasy worlds were quite real and even up to the most modern of times there have been a belief in faeries and elves and their kin.

Faeries have remained popular throughout time as writers spun their tales of their wonder and artists painted their perceived images.

We look back on familiar tales such as Cinderella with her faerie godmother or the comedy of William Shakespeare's "A Midsummer Night's Dream" to find faeries in literature. The Grimm Brothers brought us many a tale of magical beings, as well as Hans Christen Anderson with his The Little Mermaid among other stories. While Disney took this tale and added music and a happy ending, the Grimm Brothers often brought a darker side to the land of magical beings.

As we study more about the legends and mythology of the world of the faerie, we find there was a darker side to the land of fey. Those that believed in the realm of faeries – especially those who lived in Great Britain – would speak of tales where humans could be kidnapped by the faeries and would often even mate with humans.

For a long while, faeries weren't quite the benevolent beings we think of today. Instead they were something to be feared. Many a tale of kidnapped human was told and people were warned to stay away from places that the faerie people populated.

Yet there were many people who still believed that faeries were good. They pointed to the beauty of the land and announced that Mother Nature had to have help to create such beauty.

Then of course there was the magical aspect of these mysterious beings. Leprechauns had gold; faeries could cast spells of beauty and brownies could help clean your home. So the myths and tales continued through the ages.

Writers continued to popularize and feed the belief. Today's children know of the Blue Fairy who appears in the tale of Pinocchio. J.R. Tolkien writes about the world of faeries in his Lord of the Ring series of books. And of course at Christmas, Santa Claus would be nowhere without his many elves. Elves are also part of the faerie realm.

The world of magical beings date back into time and their tales come from around the world. But many of these beings have been categorized by various mythological and historical writers as being part of the faerie realm, which is part of the angelic realm. Thus faeries are referred to as nature's angels.

For many years, the belief in these beings were delegated only to the pages of popular children's literature and the occasional fireside ghost story or mythological tale; but there has always been an underlying need of people who wanted to truly believe that this faerie magical realm was real. And that belief came to a very real possibility in Great Britain during the early 1900's.

It was at the height of the spiritualism movement during the later part of the 19th century and early 20th century, that faeries began to be really popular once more. This was a time when skeptics of ghosts and other otherworldly mysteries fell away as the world of the medium and crystal ball, flying trumpets and table tipping became popular. People were more inclined to believe in magic, because they believed in ghosts.

In 1904, playwright Sir James Barrie presented a new London stage play: "Peter Pan", whose instant success spurred a renewed interest in faeries, since one of its main character, Tinkerbell held the adult and child audience's keen interest. Barrie followed the popular stage play with a book version of the story in 1915 –again keeping the interest in this magical world continuing.

Other authors and artists began to spin their own fairy tales about faeries. Perhaps it was one of these books, full of faerie illustrations that sparked the imagination of two cousins, who lived in the English countryside village of Cottingly.

Between 1917 and 1921, the frenzy over faeries grew to a fever pitch and the media went ballistic as the news broke about

two English countryside cousins, who claimed to have taken photographs of real faeries.

The girls claimed that they had captured images of real faeries on film and they showed off these photographs to the neighboring public. The story got picked up by the press and soon media frenzy was going on.

With the type of press we give to today's movie star or celebrity, there was a similar fervor about this wondrous event, of the photographed proof of faeries. They really did exist; at least they existed in England – where even today the belief in faeries remains high, so the media cried out and sold many a newspaper.

Photography was still considered a novelty for many and was still considered at its infancy at the turn of the twentieth century. This might have been the reason that the public was taken in so easily by a series of 'actual' photographs of faeries taken by the two girls who seemed to convince the world with their 'real' photographs of faeries.

The great Cottingly faerie pictures were "authenticated" by known scientists at the time and while many didn't believe in the faerie photos, there were many who did seemed to be fooled by the photos. Even Sir Arthur Conan Doyle, author of the Sherlock Holmes series, got caught up in the zeal about the possibility of real faeries, which ran rabid at the time because of the newspaper photos of the girls interacting with what appeared to be faeries.

The Cottingly cousin faerie frenzy lasted over three years, with many believing long after that time.

But when the cousins grew up and were older, both admitted to having faked the photos. Disappointment and probably embarrassment passed through the English countryside. Thus the cousins' admittance finally ended the great controversy about the famous Cottingly faerie photos, which had played out over such a long time.

Today those photographs, the camera they used and the cutouts they posed are now in a British museum. If you search for Cottingly photos on the web, you will be able to see these photographs for yourself.

Looking at these photos today, one can easily see the flatness of the pictures of faeries compared to the girls' three dimensional images. But the frenzy took place when photography was still young and the belief in faeries was fueled by the media and by the popular culture at the time.

People want to believe in faeries, in magic and in the possibility of enchantment. This belief still remains with us.

The Walt Disney Company has produced many a film with faeries in them, from Cinderella to Sleeping Beauty. Other film makers have added their own tales to the mix aiding in the belief of faeries and the magic they hold.

Today New Age believers as well as those who practice the ancient earth religions embrace the possibility of faeries.

There has sprung up a mini-industry around these beliefs that include annual events where faery believers come together and celebrate the magic of Mother Nature. Many people love to dress in faery costumes during these events. There are also magazines whose sole purpose is to promote the belief in faeries.

Adding to all of this, are the many fantasy artists and writers who also help to keep the belief of faeries alive and strong with wonderful paintings and drawings of faeries, as well as myriad of both fiction and non-fiction books, games and figurines of faeries. People will put faeries statues in their gardens to help their garden grow.

Then there are the various individuals and groups who teach about the world of Mother Nature's invisible helpers, including yours truly who also learned to believe.

The myths and legends of old continue to fuel the real possibility of magic today. If only you believe....

Chapter Four:
You Must Believe in Us

Faeries need for us to believe in them. For they live in the ethereal world, in an existence half in our world and half in theirs. They are unlike angels in this manner, although they are part of the angelic realm. Their bodies are denser than other higher vibrational beings, such as angels. This is the reason it is possible to see faeries – if you have their permission and you are sensitive enough to their vibration.

Faeries are the guardian angels of nature including plants, animals and minerals. They are concerned with Mother Nature and the care of the planet we call Earth.

As we humans are thinking more about 'going green' and global warming, pollution and the way we treat our planet, we should be opening ourselves up to the faerie world and all that they bring to us. For the faeries help the planet thrive and by helping them, we also help the planet.

Now is the time of the faerie. As we continue in our world where such social, cultural and economic changes continue daily, tapping into the faerie realm may aid in our dealings with these global changes. Faeries can offer healing to humans and animals. They also love romantic pursuits, offer a culture of peace and harmony and respect each other and work together a team for the betterment of their existence. All powerful aspects of life we could do better at. By studying their world, we can improve ours.

Faeries are here to help us learn more about the physical natural world we live in and exist with every day. They are an important part in the structure of nature and if we listen carefully we can learn much from these diminutive creatures of light and love.

To help keep them in our world and to interact with the various flora and fauna, we can add to their abilities by lending belief and love to their important mission. That is why it is important to accept these beings as part of our otherworldly reality. Just as we believe in angels and spirit guides, so we should believe in the faerie realm and make it part of our spiritual belief system.

The angels work with the faerie realm which has its own hierocracy with a variety of individualized beings such as sprites, brownies, elves and such, all of which rule over various aspects of nature. Together these beings are called "elementals" for they interact with the elements of earth.

After my first adventure with the faeries in my bedroom, I started to allow myself to see them. I would ask them to reveal themselves to me while sitting in my living room. I wouldn't see anything at first, but while watching television, I would note from the corner of my eye, the occasional burst of tiny light.

The more I paid attention to these phenomena, the more it would occur. I experimented to make sure I wasn't seeing something else – like floaters in my eyes behind my contact lenses, or reflective lights from stray headlights or other more common reasons for tiny bursts of light. I ruled out these common elements and reasons, and soon I was able to see the tiny lights that are a sign of faerie energy.

It helped that I had live plants in my apartment, along with some crystals – all are natural and this is where faerie folk like to hang out. It also helped that I was psychically aware and that I had angels and high spirit guides that I normally hung out with. Beings of this nature seem to like other beings of this nature. It's the old like attracts like principal.

I began to get a feel for their presence and I continued to learn more about the creatures from books. I learned that many feel that faeries are mischievous – hiding items and allowing them to mysteriously re-appear again, for example. And soon items were disappearing from my home too!

I learned that some people felt that the faeries were tricksters and one had to be careful for you could easily offend them.

A run of bad luck started soon after I began to interact with the faeries and I soon decided that the books I read were right. My interest in faeries was best left behind and so I turned away from their help and their perceived trickery.

I turned again to my angels and spirit guides for help and my life began to pick back up in numerous ways. The years passed. I moved from my apartment in Oak Park when I got a corporate job in northern Illinois as a computer analyst. I lived in southern Wisconsin for a time, until I built a home with a large back yard. I opened and closed a retail New Age book and gift store. I became a certified crystal healer and a spiritual teacher.

Eventually, I got laid off from my corporate job and then got hired on again as a contractor. My beloved cat Sammy passed but other new beloved cats joined the family and my social circle picked up to include many friends and acquaintances. My sister and I got closer as our mother passed away. One year, I traveled to the west and learned to speak to the mountains. Time was good to me as I continued to heed the guidance of my angels.

But the subject of faeries would come up periodically and as I sat at my dining room table one night with a friend, discussing the creatures, I saw one dart among the artificial flowers on the table.

"Did you see that?" I declared excitedly. She had seen it, she said with a smile. But she was prone to see faeries as she had learned and believed in them since she was a child. There were other friends who also believed and yet my reluctance to connect with the faeries further continued.

Ah, all things in their own time, the faeries tell me now.

In my home in northern Illinois, at some point I got the gardening bug. Now I figured out long ago that I could grow indoor plants and flowers. I'm real good with geraniums, both inside and out. I was good with potted plants – but a garden? My reluctance to dig in the dirt was prevalence to belief in faeries again.

My mother was a gardener. She grew roses with ease and plants and flowers of every color and variety. Wherever we lived, I remember having a huge garden that my mother enjoyed tremendously. My sister got my mother's green thumb and from a young age learned how to garden, along side of my mother.

Today my sister's garden is small due to the small yard they have, but her garden too is stocked full of roses, herbs, vegetables and many types of flowers, crammed into every nook and cranny.

Both women are wonderful gardeners and over the years they have attempted to drag me into the gardening scene. My sister thought she had succeeded when I moved into my suburban home with its large backyard. But digging in the dirt wasn't something I liked to do. I found no fun bending over, digging out garden patches or pulling weeds. From the start, I hired a lawn maintenance person to cut and maintain my yard.

Then I got laid off and found myself working from home, with time to spend on my back patio. And I began to want more from my green grass – I wanted more color. I had managed to get some trees planted – friends will tell you that I love trees – but now I needed and wanted more color. So reluctantly, at first, I picked up a shovel and began to dig. And I found I liked it!

Much to my surprise, I found I liked to garden as I began to connect with the earth. And I began to plant. I planted roses that came back up the following year. I planted annuals and learned I should have planted perennials. I grew tomatoes with success. I even grew huge pumpkins one year.

My sister gave me day lilies, which are really easy to grow. My garden was coming alive with color and texture and I liked digging garden patches. I lost weight, so bending over wasn't so much of a problem. I still had my lawn maintenance people pull the weeds though!!

I found gardening…and as a result the faeries found me — again. I had been teaching angel workshops during the last couple of years and now the faeries wanted equal time. They wanted their own workshop and their own introduction into the human world.

Now is the time for the faerie realm to come back into the world – when people are becoming increasingly aware of their environment again. Now is the time, when the belief in angels is so strong.

Over 80% percent of the US population believes in angels. Much less believe in faeries, but I am rapidly learning that they can be just as strong an ally. And that they aren't as much of a trickster or mischievous as some would have us believe.

Instead they are loving nature creatures here to help our planet. It is time we learn to connect with them once again.

Chapter Five:
Now is the Time

The book had been sitting on my shelf for years. I had tried to pick it up and read it more than once but the timing wasn't right. Now the time was here. The faeries wanted a workshop and I needed to learn about them. So I picked up the book and began to read.

I was amazed at what I read and what I learned. This was a different look at the faerie realm that I had read about in my first encounter with a real faerie world. Immediately I took the knowledge from this new book and began to apply it to my life and immediately I began to connect with the faerie realm.

I grew calmer, more relaxed, less harried and worried. I began to view the world with fresh eyes. I become more creative and I saw a brighter future ahead of me.

The knowledge I learned from the book that had sat on my book shelf for ages, was amazing and far reaching for me. It was the result of the newfound creativity that resulted in this book that you are reading now. It was within the pages of international author and angel expert, Dr. Doreen Virtue's book "Healing with Faeries" that I came to realize that faeries were truly real and not to be feared.

So I have to thank the faeries for coming to Dr. Virtue who wrote the book that sat on my bookshelf for so long unread. Isn't it great when we finally do get inspired to pick up that book and read it? Do you think the faeries had any say in the matter? I do.

I finished reading Dr. Virtue's book in two days and learned much about her own adventure with the faeries and her own special faerie tale. I learned more about what it means to be a celebrity – for this is what I think of when I think of Doreen Virtue. She is what I want to be – an expert speaker/teacher and writer. I know I am on my way.

I actually met Dr. Virtue—albeit briefly and only in passing. Dr. Doreen Virtue (and yes, she says that is her real name) has a doctoral degree in psychoanalysis and specializes in nutrition. Her many books tell her tale of how she moved from that occupation to becoming an angel expert and author. I met her one summer at the International New Age Trade Show (INATS) in Denver, Colorado.

INATS is a trade show where professional artists, authors and musicians along with many other retail vendors meet with retailers, each buying and selling to each other. I knew that Doreen Virtue would be there; I had wanted to attend her special speaking session, but wasn't able to due to prior commitments. But as I was rushing to and fro, from exhibit hall to exhibit hall, I looked up and saw this rather tall, elegant looking blonde woman, who quite frankly looked like an angel. I could almost see her wings, her aura was so angelic. Just as I was almost passed her, I realized who she was --Doreen Virtue. I'm pleased to say that she noticed me and nodded with a smile.

I wished I could have talked with her, although at the time I hadn't read her "Healing with Faeries" book. I had read some of her angel books however. These book lend themselves to unique insights to this woman, who I think of as a celebrity. As it turns out, despite her success, she's just as insecure and unsure as the rest of us about many things in her life. Or she was when she wrote many of her earlier books. When I read her "Healing with Faeries" book, I learned that it was the faeries that helped her through one of her greatest times of need.

Life can be one of insightful challenges and after reading Doreen's book; I knew it was the faeries that were to be my next acceptance on the magical carpet ride of my spiritual journey.

For me, they were the next progression as my own life opened to new territories and challenges. I learned from Dr. Virtue as much as I learned from the faeries; there seemed, at least for me, to be a logical progression from angels' wisdom to faeries' guidance.

I bring this knowledge forward to the reader, for in revealing my own journey, perhaps you can relate while traveling on your journey. We are all connected and the Creator sits high above (metaphorically speaking) and watches over us and guides us along. He has sent helpers and they are the angels and now the faeries.

Now is the time for us to step forward on our spiritual path and embrace the many gifts these wonderful beings have to offer us all.

Chapter Six:
Taking the First Steps

The first step one has to complete before you can possibly see or hear one from the faerie world is to believe. Belief is key and helps you connect with their world. Belief from humans aids and empowers the faeries.

The second step is step outside into the world of nature, for this is the faeries domain. They are part of nature and have been called nature's angels. In the hierarchy of the heavens and other worlds, it is the angels who rule and guard over the faerie world.

The mission and purpose of the faeries and their kin are to maintain balance in the Earth's environment and tend to Mother Nature's blessings.

There are four different aspects of nature and thus four different types of faeries. Those aspects are: air, water, fire and earth. Each of these aspects has their own set of individual faeries attached to them.

For each element there is a type of elemental being, ultimately ruled by an archangel. There are astrological signs that are also attached to the different elements. Finding your sign may help you to connect with a particular type of elemental.

Use the chart to find your sun sign and then read the description of the elemental and see how the two coincide in your life.

Do you find similarities to your own traits and personality?

Elementals Classifications			
Element	**Elemental Being**	**Angel**	**Zodiac Signs**
Earth	Gnomes	Ariel	Taurus Virgo Capricorn
Water	Undines	Gabriel	Cancer Scorpio Pisces
Air	Sylphs	Raphael	Gemini Libra Aquarius
Fire	Salamanders	Michael	Aries Leo Sagittarius

Earth Elementals

Those elementals associated with the earth include other beings than strictly faeries. They include gnomes, dwarves, trolls and elves. From Ireland, they include the leprechauns, from Britain come the brownies and in Germany are the kobold. They also include the nature spirits who reside in trees and bushes, as well as the flower, garden and field faeries.

In our modern mythology, when we think of faeries, they are usually earth elemental faeries. They assist in helping the Earth energies and have dominion over the ground, rocks, crystals and minerals, plants and animals. Their category is Gnome, but they comprise of many types of faerie beings.

Because we as humans are comprised of both minerals and water, we rely heavily on the earth elementals. These gnomes help us remain grounded and help us assimilate earth energies including materials taken from the earth that we eat, including our vitamins and minerals. They help us with endurance and our physicality on this earth plane.

They help to remind us of the beauty of nature and allow us to be playful and to be appreciative of what the Earth provides for us.

If we look inside ourselves and embrace our own personal gnome, we can allow ourselves to be more fully alive and become one with Mother Nature.

Water Elementals

Again we remind ourselves that we as humans are composed of both minerals and water. Thus the water elementals play another important role in our lives.

The water elemental, whose category is labeled Undines, consists of water sprites, nymphs as well as mermaids. Dolphins are closely linked with the water elementals as are frogs and other small amphibians.

We must have water in our lives and the water elementals work with us on several levels. Water — wherever it may be – whether in oceans, streams, rivers, lakes, brooks or in the rain—have undine activity. Water is a source of healing energy and is often associated with emotions and feminine energies.

Undine energy is thought to help us waken our emotions and allow us to release those emotions when needed in times of crisis, sorrow as well as in joy and happiness. They have the power of creation, of flow, of imagination and creativity. They help us unlock these aspects in ourselves as well as unlocking the aspects of the sexual being within each of us.

You'll find water elementals in all types of water, but also in dreams – for fluid motion and dimensional shifting is their specialty.

Too little undine energy in your life will stifle creativity; too much can cause a water well of overflowing emotions. Balance is always the key.

Air Elementals

We must breathe to live and the air elementals help us on all levels with the air we breathe and live in. These sylphs work directly with our guardian angels and help protect and serve us in many ways include working with children and healers.

They help us with our function of breathing but remind us that we must stop and smell the roses too. They help us gain knowledge and insight into our lives as we remember to breathe deeply of life.

They often serve as temporary guardian angels until we step up in vibration to accept those higher vibrational beings into our lives. They assist children who have passed over and aid in helping animals and firefighters, as well as ambulance workers.

Where ever there is oxygen, there is an air elemental at work, reminding us to breathe deep and often in our spiritual quest and personal life journey.

Fire Elementals

The sun is the giver of life and what is the sun? It is fire, which provides light to us. Thus we must have fire – for it provides us with both light and warmth.

Fire feeds us from within too – it fuels our passions and our creativity. This is the purpose of the fire elemental – the salamanders – whose flames dance and spit at us where ever fire burns.

Light a candle or watch a fire and you'll see these elementals shoot out from the flames and dance in the air. They are perhaps the easiest of the elementals to see.

 We connect with the fire elementals whenever we feel intense emotions including love, passion and even hatred and anger. The fire elemental can fuel us in a creative way or destructively. We must be careful that they don't consume us completely.

The salamanders named perhaps for the spits of fire, which look like a lizard's forked tongue, are associated with the fire signs of the zodiac.

We need fire in our bellies to move us forward and so the fire elementals help us with our passions. With them, we can dare to dream the bigger dreams and create great buildings, cures, movies, bridges and so much more.

If you dream big, then your personal salamander has done its job.

When and where do you find faeries when you are outside?

The best times for spotting these tiny creatures are in the twilight times or the 'in between' times – those times that are neither day nor night. These times include dawn and dusk, midnight and noon, during the days before and after the new moon and the full moon. These are in between times for dawn is neither night nor day yet; dusk is no longer day, but not really night. Noon and midnight have the same type of qualities, while the moon phases are not quite full or not quite new.

"There is magic to these times and they have been mystical to mankind since the beginning of time. The shadow times are half hazy and shadows blend and wave into fantastic shapes. Now is the time that dimensional portals will open and close," the faeries whisper to me.

On my desk are two large crystals and several small pieces of crystal. One is a large clear quartz piece and the other is a chunk of amethyst. Then there are smaller pebbles of pink quartz and black tourmaline, plus a few other pieces of clear quartz.

One of the things that excite me about the faerie realm is learning that crystals and minerals also fall into this category.

As a certified crystal healer – which means I utilize crystals and minerals as tools for energy healing—it was a natural progression for me to learn more about their place in the hierarchy of nature devas.

Crystals and minerals can talk to us with the nature devas who guard over them. It is the individual power of the stone that

merges with our energy field to heal and cleanse it; it is the stone's deva who nourishes the soul. Together they make a wonderful and powerful duo to life and rebuild energy, to clean, heal and balance us at a molecular level.

At work, with my job at corporate America, I keep meaning to bring in a live plant or two. Often the energies at work, due to the nature of the corporate atmosphere, can get stuck. I have noticed too often that when I am at work, with its myriads of meetings and deadlines, I can easily get caught up in the work mentality frenzy. Not a good thing for any one, but as a person who tries to stay calm and peaceful, it definitely isn't good for me. Which is why I thought a nice plant would help with the energies of my cubicle. I have yet to find a good one to bring in.

In the meantime however, I have hung several pictures of nature. I also have a small stuffed angel teddy bear on my desk. Plus I stick a piece of clear quartz and some amethyst under my computer monitor. I believe all these items help me connect with the faerie realm and so I can hear them whispering to me now and then—even at work.

Faeries are shy creatures and because man has been so destructive to their homes, they distrust humans. We pollute the Earth; tear down forests, and up root farms lands to put up our cities, towns, shopping malls and subdivisions. We do this all without asking their permission or blessing the land beforehand. This displaces the faeries and destroys their homes. They look on helpless as we pollute the air and the land. We litter the ground with trash.

The faerie realm asks us to change our ways to save the Earth from global warming and melting icecaps. They ask us to help them pick up the litter, so they can heal that which has been damaged by the litter. They ask us to be kind to the animals that they are in charge of – the wild and free as well as the domestic beasts and creatures of the land.

"Please take care of the land; love it as we do and we all will be better for the efforts," the faeries speak. *"Love the land as we do and we will work with you."*

If you want to connect with the faerie realm, you must learn to bridge the gap of trust. Re-establish that which has been broken so often. Let them learn to trust you and know that you care about their world – which is your world too.

When you are out in the world of nature, whether it is in a park, a forest preserve, on a beach or in your backyard, respect the land. Pick up trash where you find it; begin to recycle. Warn the faeries and ask them for their permission when you begin to dig in the garden or even mows the grass. Let them know you plan to walk among their midst and give them time to move out of the way.

Don't dig up toadstools without warning—these are homes to elves, brownies and leprechauns. The flowers are home to the field and flower faeries. Work with them and they will reward you with magnificent blooms, visits from helpful animals and the song of birds that can lift the hearts of all who care to listen.

While their world is invisible, it is made of denser material than the angels. They are close to our world dimensionally, which allows us to peek into their world.

Once the faeries know that they can trust you this world can become visible to you.

 Where do you begin to look? Your own backyard may be a good start, but the faerie world is a dimensional portal away from ours and this is where it is best to look. Again it is where there are places of in-between: crossroads, beaches, tide pools, islands, and hills – all are known portal entrances to the land of the fey.

How do we know if we are connecting with the faerie realm?

There are signs that they are nearby and are attempting to make contact with humans. We need not see them to know they are nearby.

A gentle breeze when the air is still; the fragrance of a flower; the stirring of a pool of water when there is no wind or the

bending of a grass stem – all are signs that the faeries are near and watching.

Signs of Nature That Show We Are Connecting....

1. A gentle breeze, a whisper of leaves stirring

2. Bending of grass blends without cause

3. The stirring of dust into a dust devil

4. A sudden chill in the air dancing along your shoulders as you take a walk along a forest path

5. Seeing ripples in water when there is no breeze or fish

6. A sudden case of the giggles or fit of laughter

7. Losing time

8. Feeling something brush against your skin, tickle your scalp

9. Walking in a field and feeling as if spider webs touch your face

10. The gathering of birds and a burst of song

11. Insects such as bees appearing and dancing among flowers when they were none before

12. The feeling of being watched when alone in nature....

There are ways and methods of allowing the faeries to know you wish to connect with them. The experience with any of the elementals is subtle; their energy is very gentle. Here is a list of ways to start to connect:

1. Spend time outdoors in nature. Take regular walks in parks, in gardens and along the seashore.

2. Meditate while sitting under a tree or near a lake. Or near a babbling brook or stream.

3. Ask the faeries to come forth with a gentle prayer.

4. Grow live plants and flowers indoors and nurture them with kindness and loving ways.

5. Keep the clutter out of your home – faeries don't like clutter.

6. Let your yard have a place to grow wild plants and flowers. Let the faeries play undisturbed in their special place.

7. Build a faerie house in their special place. An old decorative birdhouse will do nicely.

8. Become more creative and playful in everyday living.

9. Play music – gentle and soothing sounds will gain their attention.

10. Learn to sing – faeries love music and singing.

11. Respect Mother Nature and help clean up the planet. Learn to recycle!

12. Be nice to others and generous when asked – you never know when a Faerie will take human form and ask a favor!

13. Allow yourself to awaken the child in you – for it is the children who first welcome and recognize the Faerie world and help keep it alive!

14. Read about faeries – and put yourself into a famous story. Weave a magic tale with yourself as the hero or heroine.

15. Volunteer at an animal shelter.

16. Have a picnic with a loved one near a stream or forest. Faeries love romance!

These are but just a few methods to start connecting with the faerie realm. You can come up with more! Be playful and be creative!

Chapter Seven:
The Power of Faeries

We touched upon some of the benefits of faeries in our lives. They are the caretakers of nature, the animals, plants and minerals are their kingdoms.

But once we gain their trust and they become our friends, they can help us as we help them. We help by being kind to ourselves, others, animals and to nature.

They help us by allowing our inner child to play, to bestow upon us good luck and allow magic back into our lives.

They are indeed magical beings with what we would think of as magical powers, which include the following:

1. Levitation
2. Invisibility
3. Glamour
4. Shape-shifting
5. Creative craftsmanship
6. Wonderful musicians
7. Control over the weather
8. Healers
9. Ability to instill sleep or altered states of consciousness

Faeries can cast what is called a "glamour" – a power to shift how others see themselves and the world. The faeries cast a "spell" over a person that shows the person what the faeries want them to see. For example, if a person is handsome, the faeries can cause the person to see themselves as ugly – or vice versa – a homely individual can be caused to see their reflection as a thing of beauty.

Faeries also can appear and disappear at will. They will often shape-shift into a form of an animal – a bird or a frog. This shape-shifting ability is played out in many a faerie tale and this is also where the princesses kissing a frog stem from.

Faeries can also take human forms when they so choose; something that was much more common several centuries ago then today. But one never knows where or when one might come across a faerie in human form...especially a faerie godmother!

The tale of Cinderella and her faerie godmother is as popular today as it ever was, but this tale has more truth to it than not. For it is said that there are those [faeries] who will take on human form, simply to test humans and their generosity.

That old woman who asks for help carrying groceries or an old homeless crone asking for a quarter might just be a faerie who could grant you a wish – if your heart is generous and your intentions are true and honest.

It is said that nature spirits ask us not to take things for granted. They often will bestow simple gifts of stone, feathers or flowers to those who they favor. Accept these with the intent they were given, thank the nature spirits for their gifts and good luck will be given. But turn away such a gift and there may be a price to pay.

Chapter Eight:
Connecting with the Faeries

One of the reasons I believe I got more excited about faeries is that one year, in my front yard, I found a faerie ring.

A faerie ring is a place where the grass grows into a distinct ring of a darker color. It is said that often a ring of toadstools may grow around the perimeter and often the ring will grow akin to a hill or slope of the land. The faerie ring serves as a portal to the faerie world. Step inside the ring, or dare fall asleep inside, especially during the in between times and one will no doubt be escorted to the world of the fey, so we are told.

Many myths and tales exist surrounding such faerie rings and dimensional portals, where humans fall folly into a world where they may never be returned. The passage of time on the faerie side is different than the human world. A human living in the faerie realm can live there for years and then return to the human world and find it's only been a few hours later. Maybe no one even knew they were gone!

Of course, just the opposite is also true – a few days in the world of the faerie, may turn into years in the human world. This could be troublesome indeed – finding that you didn't age while all around you others did!

I can't say I fell into any portal, for I was careful not to step inside my faerie ring that grew that summer on a slope in my front yard. It was a distinct different shade of grass and a ring of toadstools that clearly marked the spot.

Even my neighbor, a total non-believer in anything remotely magical, was surprised to see the ring appear again after he mowed my grass. I warned the faeries when he mowed and perhaps this was the reason I was so graced by this wondrous faerie ring, even after several mowing cycles.

While I would have loved to leave the yard not mowed, my city's ordinances do not allow such doings and so each time I warned the faeries. Finally the mowing season was over and the ring faded with the summer sun.

The next year I looked for the ring to appear again, but alas it did never did reappear, although some new sections of clover did appear. This was the only experience I had with a faerie ring, thus far.

I did take several photos of the ring though and these I share with you. Look for these types of rings in your own yard and if you must mow, please warn the faeries ahead of time. It takes time and effort to build such a ring.

But be cautious of stepping inside or you might be whisked away to a faerie land!

My Faerie Ring

The faerie ring in my front yard

I was blessed by the faeries.

"When or if you find a faery ring in your yard you know you're being watched and blessed by the faery realm. Now would be a good time to start a garden, feed the birds, do yard cleaning and make sure you recycle. When we love Mother Earth, she loves us back." – Queen Jejaia, Faerie Queen to the Northeast Illinois faerie kingdom.

Can you find the faeries?

It was shortly after the faerie ring appeared that the faeries introduced themselves to me. They became insistent that I write a book and also teach classes about faeries and their mission.

The book that they compelled me to write is the one you are now reading, my first non-fiction book. The classes I taught used this book's material as a workbook and part of the class was taught outside.

I had managed prior to teaching the class and while writing the book to truly connect more with the faerie realm of my backyard.

In my research I learned that faeries often are set up in monarch structure with faery kings and queens that rule individual kingdoms.

Because I am a person who speaks with angels, it wasn't hard for me to connect with the faerie kingdom of my area, especially after the faerie ring appeared. There is quite a lot of this book that has been dictated to me by the Faerie Queen Jejaia, who is the resident monarch of my backyard in northern Illinois.

She provided direction on what and how to teach a faerie class, which I continue to do today, usually in the spring and summer months.

But by my first class I hadn't truly connected with Queen Jejaia face to face. Instead we had talked telepathically. However, that was about to change, as I taught the class how to connect with the faerie realm, by traveling to my back yard.

Exercises to Connect with the Faeries

We now step outside, beach towel or blanket in hand to connect with the faeries. Bring along a camera too for a faerie may make herself known to you!

Our workshop indoors was complete as we finished our books and came to this section. It was time to go outside and connect with the faeries as they had promised to do so, if I wrote the book and held the workshop. So outside we went.

We lay in the backyard on towels and blankets and closed our eyes, breathing deeply, under the brilliant blue sky and warm summer sun. Our heart rates now slower and we let our minds wander momentarily, taking in the sounds of the dragonflies and the sound of the birds. These noises grew around us and we knew from the lessons learned, that the faeries were afoot.

It felt good to feel them nearby and it felt as if I were the giant among the tiny beings who were now throwing their invisible threads of healing energy over me, forming a woven energy web. I could almost feel the threads, the tiny prickling around my shoulders and scalp, around my bare feet. My toes tickled. Spider webs of ethereal energy were cast about my face. I began to relax.

Deeper and deeper I went under until I was among the flowers themselves. I sat on a stalk of tall grass and looked up to see a beautiful regal female complete with wings that resembled dragonflies and in a gown of spun gold. Her hair was like sunshine and she smiled at me with a wry but knowing grin of satisfaction. I knew this person – this being—she was Jejaia (pronounced Je-Ji-ya)– who had come to me and helped me write my book. She was the one that wanted me to have the faerie class. She had urged me to write a book instead of presenting the class material with my usual Power Point presentation.

Here she was in front of me and I almost felt the need to bow in her royal presence; for she was the Faerie Queen of my backyard.

"Hello," I addressed her with a nod of my head.

"*Welcome,*" she answered, and then thanked me for the class.

"I'm honored. Thank you for the faerie ring."

That was their sign she said; I was being tested. And would be...for now was the time for humans with abilities such as mine to come into their own power and behold a world beyond their own limited sights, sounds and feelings. I had begun to become accepted as I continued to nurture the land and take care of the animals. (I had four cats at the time and had found a home for a lost cat the year before.)

But as a teacher, healer and a channel, not to mention writer, I was in particular need of getting the word out. I was a light worker and the faeries worked with our kind to help spread the word about the earth, the environment and about their existence, in a variety of methods. She thanked me for accepting the challenge.

I felt honored, as we talked briefly more; her voice carried weight and authority. Her manner was friendly but reserved. She came across as a being of power.

All too soon, it was time to come out of my mediation and the energy web I felt before was now gone, either absorbed or removed, I'm uncertain which. I blinked against the light of the sun and shared my adventure with the others. They too felt the energy webs, the exalted sounds of nature and felt more relaxed and at peace.

Messages from faerie oracle cards had brought special meanings to each student and later we would compare the photos we took of the field and the flowers, hoping to catch a faerie at work or play. We had asked their permission before hand – something that must be done to catch a glimpse of their magical world.

I had shared my channeled messages with them – reiterating the need to honor their world and our own environment and earth.

Each of us now had a special memory of that sunny day, as we began to connect with the faeries. Our journeys have just begun!

Could faeries be hiding here?

Chapter Nine:
The Adventure Continues

My adventures with the faeries didn't end in my backyard that afternoon. During the course of the next several years, my adventures with the realm of the fey continued.

I finished the faerie book, but it remained in a different, more hand-made format, than it does now. Technology has helped me bring this information into the world years after that first class.

Life continued on for me after that first class and while the class went well, life had different plans for me. I sprained my knee one year soon after and that was the end of gardening for me. Fortunately it wasn't the end of my interaction with the faerie world.

I learned that faeries don't just live outdoors. If you have living plants in your home, they will use these plants to make their indoor home.

Faeries in the home must be respected. For they indeed can be mischievous—more times than I can count did my keys turned up missing. I finally had to ask the faeries to either stop or leave. After that the keys didn't get misplaced so easily. Lesson learned.

The good news was my once brown thumb had turned green with the faeries' help with my many indoor plants. The plants now flourished and grew.

An Elf Shows Up

One day in my back yard, I was taking photos of the various flora and fauna. I contacted the local kingdom and asked if I could perhaps get a picture of a faerie. When I came towards one of my rose bushes, the answer was clear as a bell to take a picture— at that very moment—as in "now".

I snapped the picture and low and behold – not a faerie— but an elf showed up in the photo! I was not only a bit astonished, but really was pleased too. Of course I thanked the faeries by leaving little treats around the faerie house I had for them in my garden. I've included the photo here, but as I proofed this book, I found the photography doesn't really show the elf well.

You can find the color photograph also on our website at: www.TheAngelicPath.com.

Can you find the elf's top of the head in this picture?
See circle on the picture to find it better!

You can see the elf in the circle.

If you look closely, you will see the top of his head, his ear and the tip of his nose. He's looking down towards the leaf of the rose (left bottom corner). Again, he is a dimensional being and so while it might be a trick of the light for the non-believer—I know that he's real. The photo of course is the original and has not been retouched in any manner! Again – the book photo might not really show the detail. Travel to the web to get a better look at the color photograph.

Of course I was thrilled to get such a photo for faeries are shy. They don't exactly pose for pictures.

With the advent of digital cameras and smart phones, we do have more opportunities since we carry these technological wonders with us everywhere now. It's much easier to take a quick a picture now than it was just a few years back. And many have access to photo editing computer programs, so be cautious claiming you have a photo of a faerie...people these days aren't as naïve and willing to believe as in the days when the Cottingly cousins snapped their faerie pictures!

Trees and Rock Spirits

Over the next few years, I learned more about the spirits in the trees. On a field trip with other nature loving spiritual students, we found a park that held many trees that had knots and bumps in their bark that resembled faces. We could feel the energy of these trees and saw there was something more than meets the eye.

I found out that faeries will often hide within these special trees. If you find a tree with unusual bark formations or root formations, watch for openings in the trunk or around the roots. For here is where faeries will often make their natural home.

Be careful not to disturb them, but you might want to leave a treat or two (they love small hard candies or M&Ms) for them and perhaps they will grant you a favor or a blessing.

See the small hole just above the ring? Could this be a faerie home?

I had to leave Queen Jejaia's kingdom and the back yard where my faery ring had grown. Alas, it never did come back after that summer.

In the neighborhood I live in now, I am surrounded by wild prairie land, with many trees in my backyard and around me. These trees hold special magic in them – I know I am protected by their energy.

My backyard in Wisconsin

At first, the trees were cautious, for other people had come and go in the house I moved into and now rented. Trees like people who come and stay. Rocks are also particular about this movement of humans.

Learning to talk and communicate with rocks and trees was a very interesting experience for me.

Mountain rocks and boulders talk very slowly; I learned when I visited the Sandia Mountains in New Mexico.

Listening to Mountain Spirits in NM

And trees take their time warming up to you – so be patient if you so choose to talk with trees and mountains on your next hiking trip in nature.

Chapter Ten:
A Faerie Scribe Speaks with Us

Over the years, I have met many people who believe in faeries and will talk with them. So I learned I wasn't crazy to believe or talk with things one cannot typically see. This is an issue for many who want to connect to the angelic realm or non-physical being realms. I have a sign in my living room reminding me of the simple act of belief. It reads: BELIEVE. Again, it all comes down to if you can set aside your learned behaviors and have faith in something you can't see.

Faith of all types will carry you far in life. Believe that all things are possible and you will be taken care of in life. Faeries and angels and so many of our non-physical friends remind us of this in our daily lives.

So of course when I first moved into my new home, I introduced myself to the faerie kingdom of the area. And again, it took time for this realm to warm up and trust me. It didn't happen at first and it was an introduction from Queen Jejaia that finally allowed the introductions to be made.

But first I received a message from her kingdom.

Privilege Has Its Advantages

I was attempting to meditate with the trees in my back yard when I heard a voice asking me if I was ever going to do anything with my faerie book, or was it to perish on my home office book shelf.

I really hadn't thought of the book for years; I was still under the mistaken impression that getting a book published was a long arduous and expensive affair. I let the voice know as much.

It harrumphed at me and said, *"There are ways. You just don't know. Ask and you will find out."*

I have found that this is usually true and I did find out later that he was right. It took me about a year to get myself in gear to find out, but none the less he was right.

"Can I do something for you?" I asked him, changing the subject.

"Yes," he answered. *"My name is Oscar; and I am from Queen Jejaia's kingdom."*

"You're a bit away from home," I said, now curious. "Is the Queen all right?"

"She is in fine health and spirts. She bids you glad tidings."

"Please tell her hello," I said, noting that such formal language is truly part of their vernacular. Remember – faeries are most popular in Great Britain for a reason!

"I shall do so. But I am here to provide you information about our realms. Now that you live in a much larger one. It has also come to our attention, that you are teaching classes again on angels and yet not on faeries. Is this oversight on purpose?"

"No," I assured him quickly. "I plan to in the spring."

"Very good. Then would you allow me to provide you dictation about information about our realm? Perhaps you can use it in your book?"

"Sure. Of course," I answered. I was compelled back into the house to sit at my computer and take dictation from Oscar. I include it here – straight from the expert's mouth.

A Faerie Scribe Speaks

From Oscar, a scribe in Queen Jejaia's court, northeast Illinois:

"In each region there are varying sized kingdoms. While (most of the time) various areas are protected, policed, guarded and boundaries are respected, it wasn't always that way. And even today, depending on the various regions of the world where elementals reside, there are wars and battles about such matters. In this way, we are much like humans. And while we are part of the angelic kingdom, we aren't ruled by angels nor do we act like them.

First we aren't gender neutral like they are; nor as patient, loving, kind, gentle or non-judgmental. This makes us far more interesting. We enjoy our family and friends, our work and our play. Especially our friends and our play!

We interact much like humans do with almost the same set of emotions, though for some of us those emotions are more refined and others they are more extreme. It depends on the variety of the elemental or nature being. For me, being a scribe or holder of the records in our dear Queen Jejaia's court, is a pleasure and one I do with honor and respect.

We are the fey—what you call fairies or faeries—really we don't care how you spell it; although even among us are different varieties. And the fey, our preferred human description, are just one in many types of intelligent nature beings that live in a space between spaces in our world.

Our translator has written a book, which needs more information and I have been assigned to help her with this process, to explain from our point of view what nature beings are all about and what truly are the fairy tales.

Again, I will start on our regions and limit them to the North American and European continents, for that is where most of my type resides. There are others who resides elsewhere in your world, but are far enough distant to us in mannerism, social organization and disposition that humans would best not to even try to interact with these beings who are sometimes much more creature-like than being-like, if you get my drift. No insults intended—you know who you are!

Biologically speaking, they are far different too. Personally, while they do exist—not necessarily in the manner of your fairy tales and stories—you humans probably shouldn't have much to do with the mere people (mermaids, sirens, etc.), trolls, giants, ogres, etc.

Shrek aside (yes we are aware of your media and your technology), most ogres really smell bad and really do have a terrible disposition. Loathsome creatures really and sometimes I wonder how you humans managed to make a series of animated feature movies, much less a Broadway show about such beings. But I digress.

Within your own backyard lies a small part of a larger kingdom, ruled by a benevolent and loving King, Queen, Prince or Princess. Usually it is a King or Queen who rules, but as the King or Queen goes into old age (we live hundreds of years most of the time) a son or daughter may take on the duties with the elders' guidance.

This is the case in one of our neighboring kingdoms, whose sizes vary. The king's son has taken on the duties, although his father remains the true king. Our translator (Blake) has left our Queen's kingdom and has recently transferred to another kingdom, where this scenario is so. Thus our Queen has allowed me to act on our behalf in agreement with Prince Stephan and his father, King Duke. Yes, that is his name.

Once our translator is formally introduced to our monarchs, then another scribe may take my place or participate with me in our telling of our tale.

Our translator was already introduced to a far-flung kingdom in another one of your states (New York) where the ruling leader is King Aldebaran, who is a close friend of our Queen's.

Most of our leaders are good ones; they can be overthrown if they aren't. Not violently—but actually democratically. It is usually a family member who takes over; although historically that hasn't always been the case. And thus new ruling families come into the picture.

This is also why some kingdoms are larger than others. They can stretch miles or cover entire an state or states. Or they can be small—Ireland is famous for having many smaller kingdoms. Think about where we originate from and you can see why. Kingdom size can range in population from a few hundred to thousands and even millions. Think about your own cities—we are similar to this example.

Our occupations vary too but parallel your own. Although from the time our children (yes, we have those too) are young their skill sets are analyzed and they are groomed to their occupations by their natural abilities as well as their likes and dislikes.

Most of us enjoy what we do because we have an affinity towards that occupation. Therefore we are fairly happy both at home and at work. There are always exceptions to the rule, but these are few and far between.

Crime isn't a problem because everyone enjoys producing on their own and with others. We share what we have with others and there is a fair distribution of the wealth among us.

We don't all live like kings, but we don't have any homeless either. The elderly are naturally taken care of by their family. So there are no nursing homes, although there are those who help care for the young and the old.

We don't get sick too often—sickness and disease are something humans seem to want to cling to. Our frequency levels are pretty high and so disease isn't part of our vernacular. We really are a happy lot and are happy with our lot in life! If not, there is help.

Each fey being knows the importance of responsibility and is a good citizen of our kingdom. We want for nothing for we share what we have with each other.

And no, we're not into material goods, technology, etc. We are citizens of the natural world and we live and work in nature. That would be the great outdoors to you. We cooperate fully with Mother Nature and help Her with her work.

We are dimensional beings and come in a variety of sizes depending on our biological make-up. You would refer to us as having different species of the same biological being – for example you call orangutans, chimpanzees and gorillas, all monkeys.

We may call ourselves fey beings, but there are many types of us—both small and larger, more on this side of the veil than yours. Some of you have seen us and many have not.

I have a small (inches tall) being and I am able to levitate—although it is more with navigating wind currents than with wings, which I also have, but not long like some of your fairy paintings, but shorter.

But some of my kind have longer wings and are smaller or taller. Sometimes it's hard to explain—but just as you have your human races we have our different types of fey, as well as other nature beings, which you may refer to as elves, brownies and the like. We are all part of the elemental or nature kingdom though.

I hope this explanation has been sufficient to peak your interest in wanting to communicate us further. Once we trust you, communication is easy. Watch for our many signs and symbols – all nature related of course!

Remember to love and respect Mother Nature and she will love and respect you back!"

Oscar left me soon after the dictation. His information confirmed much of what I intuited already, but the privilege to receive spiritual translation from such a divine and wondrous source, never fails to amaze me.

King Duke's kingdom

Finally I received the names: King Duke and Prince Stephan – apparently rulers of this new realm in which I now lived. They knew of Queen Jejaia who apparently sent word that I could be trusted.

It was Prince Stephan who talked with me. Apparently he was the one in charge of the kingdom now, since his elderly father wasn't capable anymore but who didn't want to step down completely.

The faerie kingdom takes care of their sick and elderly; he confirmed. It is an honor to treat their people with respect and learn from their wisdom.

Prince Stephan was kind enough to accompany me on my walks in my new nature-filled neighborhood. And while technically I couldn't see him – I felt his presence and heard his voice in my head. I could feel his gestures and emotions as we talk.

"All beings have wisdom," Prince Stephan told me one day on one of our walks, *"When you start looking and really start listening to them with your heart, instead of your head. Mother Nature teaches us patience and respect. We honor humans when they do the same."* He nodded towards my recycle bin with a faint smile, when we returned home. He had learned by observation that I was now an avid recycler, separating my cardboard, plastics and other recyclable from my regular trash.

Again, the faeries are really big on recycling and taking care of Mother Nature.

Prince Stephan confirmed what Oscar had told me. There are faerie realms and kingdoms throughout the world, each ruled by a benevolent leader. The boundaries are not always clearly cut and for the most part the kingdoms are a cooperative, industrious and peace-loving group of individuals. They respect each other and work together as a team to accomplish their daily tasks in the world of nature.

They love to party, to dance and partake of merriment. They love helping humans find the joy in their lives and help them accomplish their tasks. Ask for faerie help when in the garden or when washing the dog, or when planning an outdoor wedding or party. They do enjoy helping humans who believe in them.

New York Faerie Homes

In western New York, there is a spiritualist camp and in this camp, surrounded by woods, is an area that respects and honors the faerie realm.

People from the area built and put out beautiful and quirky faerie homes. These have been built from a variety of material including wood and metal—built like miniature homes. Bits of colorful ribbons, moss, and miniature furniture complete the picture. All remain outside so the faeries can settle in.

One of the Faerie Homes

When I visited I sat on a human-sized bench that sat among the various and numerous faerie houses. I felt a special magic about the place and could feel the fey energy that surrounded the area.

While I didn't converse with any of the faeries while visiting, it was an interesting spot to say the least!

I have since attempted to take pictures of Prince Stephan's realm, but haven't seen any faeries show up yet. It takes time and patience – plus trust and belief. You've got to believe!

Once upon a time I didn't....and while the rest of the world laughs and scoffs, the magic and delight these wonderful beings can bring into one's life shouldn't be missed.

In my search for pictures of faerie homes on the web, I found a ton! Many people are building faerie homes in their gardens these days. An old bird house will do in pinch, but many have taken this art to the next level!

Do your faeries a favor and build them their own home!

Chapter Eleven:
Learning More about the Flower Faeries

It was once believed that every tree, plant and rock had its own spirit. The Native American shamans know the truth of this, as does the natural healer. But for most of us, in this technologically-laden world, such ideas are considered silly, frivolous or even anti-religious.

Such thinking in the 1600's and 1700's could have caused your death at end of a witch hunter's noose. But in the 300's and 400's A.D., such thinking was natural. Especially in what is today Great Britain where the Celts and Druids worship the world of nature and all of it's magic.

Then the Dark Ages came upon us and the world acknowledged only one spirit to worship. The age of worshipping nature was over – for the time being. Trees were meant for chopping down – for shelter and warmth and light. Flowers and herbs were simple things  to look at, but had no intrinsic value. So the Dark Ages taught man.

In man's ignorance, much has been lost. And found again. For today we enter a New Age where nature again is looked at with renewed interest and while not exactly worshipped by most, certainly many are now respecting Mother Earth.

In our examination of the faerie world, we again open ourselves up to the spirits of nature. We begin to realize that each plant, flower and tree seem to have a unique energy pattern to it.

Traditionally, man has learned from Mother Nature and many a wise woman in her day have listened carefully and learned the secrets of the flowers, the trees and the wild grasses in the field. Many of our medicines today come from Mother Nature as science has listened and learned from the wise women of old or the Native American shaman who harvested herbs, or the ancient herbalist who knew the secrets of healing. These herbs and plants serve a purpose and hold a special type of magic or energy within them. Each has their essence and spirit which seeks to heal and help.

Again we are reminded that the earth lives for us and we cannot live without her.

Flowers have been inspiration to mankind from the beginning of time. We care for flowers in magnificent gardens, hold their beauty for as long as possible in elegant vases of glass and metal, and paint their magnificence on canvas.

Photographers find the beauty of flowers especially appealing and modern light workers know well the power and energy aspects of the flower. The 1960's was amassed with the words: "Flower Power" as the Age of Aquarius was just dawning.

Much traditional lore has been built around plants and the faeries helped bring that lore into our reality.

Next time you are in the garden seek out these herbs, plants and flowers and look with new respect at their power. Find these flowers and look to the faerie family that nurtures and cares for each individual variety of flower and plant.

The information concerning each flower listed below come from a variety of recorded resources but stand on their own merit. Information was also provided by the Faerie Queen Jejaia, who helped author this book through her channeling wisdom and abilities.

Here then are some flowers and their own special fey abilities:

Angelica – Angelica as the name implies holds special power with the faeries who are nature's angels. This beautiful flower reminds us of the angelic nature of faeries and is a flower that allows humans to more fully connect to the angelic world as a whole. Angelica brings good fortune and favor.

This is a flower that allows the intuition to open and psychic abilities to strengthen. Angelica faeries have been known to leave their flower stations and follow humans home, bestowing on them good favor and temporary guardianship.

Black-Eyed Susan – This is a summer flower and as summer dawns so does great change. This is the power of the faerie of the black-eyed Susan – they are known to help enable and promote needed change in the lives of those who seek it. They shed light on dark areas of the psyche and on provide light and guidance with troubles.

Buttercup – Never was there so a compassionate faerie as those who tend to the buttercups. If you seek comfort, this is the field to lie in and tell your problems to. There are great healing energies among these faeries and they are great to boost your self-esteem and self-worth. Feeling low? The buttercup faeries are here to help!

Carnation – This is a flower of strength and immense power. The faeries will take on the color of the carnation, camouflaging themselves among the delicate petals. This way they can help humans.

Humans are drawn to specific colors that correspond with the aura – whatever selection of the aura needs healing; this is the color that the human will be drawn to. Color faeries hide among the petals and will help the human in releasing blocked energy in the human auric fields.

White carnations provide even greater healing and nourishment of strength--both physical and emotional strength healing.

Clover – This is a dwelling of the elves – who love to hide in the clover. Yes, a four-leaf clover brings good luck as does the three-leaf clover.

The clover faeries, who can be the leprechaun, will provide good-luck to those individuals who are kind to the wee folks of the bush. Watch for flicking lights, especially around the time of the full moon. White clover is an especially a powerful sign that the elfin folk are near-by.

Daisy – Queen Jejaia loves daisies. Daisies are a fun and friendly flower in the faerie realm. Here the fey aren't afraid to come and play with humans. It is a flower of vitality, long-life and strength. Put out daisies when you want the faeries to appear to you. This is an excellent flower to start with when first exploring the Faerie realm. Daisies awaken the imagination, creativity and the love of dance and promote fun.

Gardenia – These are guardian flowers, especially where children are involved. They serve as protection of both children and animals. They open psychic doors and help promote intuitive abilities. They also provide a sense of comfort and tranquility to individuals.

Geranium – These hardy flowers allow ourselves to open our hearts to ourselves and to others on both an emotional and spiritual basis. They help heal on a subtle level, working with the heart chakra. They help allow your inner being to open yourself to more adventure and joy. They provide stability and promote happiness.

Heather – A gentle breeze that promotes astral travel will heather bring, so says Queen Jejaia. There are several types of nature spirits that work with the energy of heather, for it can promote spiritual and emotional growth in humans when the human is ready and accepting of themselves. It is used on humans who have reached a level of maturity on their spiritual path.

Lilac – Lilacs are a regal flower. Their aromatic smell is a sign that spring is here. These flowers come in a variety of pink, purple, blue and white shades and the bushes are very long-lived. Rochester, New York is the Lilac Capital of the United States, where these bushes are present in almost every yard. The faeries that dwell among the lilacs are sensitive and timid. Their work is quick for lilacs only bloom for a few short weeks. Honor these faeries as they do their work by being respectful to the Mother Nature and to each other.

Rose – The rose is a romantic and regal flower with power and strength. Their petals are delicate and soft. The rose faeries treasure these petals and the smell of the rose, which can be a heady experience for human and fey alike. The faeries that guard and care for the roses are proud of their work, and rightfully so. The colors that stem forth from the rose are the faeries' work.

Delight in this flower as the faeries do.

Sage – Like its name, sage faeries are wise. This plant is home to retired faeries who aid their power to the protective quality of this plant. Sage is often burned to clear negative energies and it is this quality of the plant that the faeries aid in offering their energies to; this protective quality is joined with air faeries as this plant is burned to add to the effect.

These are the flowers that Queen Jejaia wishes those of you who are just beginning to understand the faerie folk to know about. There are many other flowers and more faeries who tend to these flowers and aid in their energies. But the flowers mentioned are the ones for beginners.

As you grow more accustom to the energies of the flower faeries, then more will be revealed to the more advanced student.

Chapter Twelve:
Learning About the Tree Faeries

Just as there are flower faeries, so are there tree spirits, as we've already mentioned. As can be imagined these are powerful beings and with power comes responsibility. The trees here allow for both the beginning fey aficionado as well as the more advanced student, a hint at the abilities that these powerful devas can dispel.

It is with respect that the human must approach the tree faeries, for their power can be overwhelming.

It would be wise to first study the trees and their lore. Go to parks and forests and spend time with trees. Learn to feel their energies and knock gently at their doors. Their secrets and powers are old and wise.

Look carefully and you will see their energy. Look further and you will see their smiling faces. In the gnarls of the wood, a face may appear or simply a set of watching eyes. Squint if wish, and ask for the tree spirit to reveal itself. If the student is ready, then the spirit will answer.

Listen for the whispers in the wind, the creak of a branch, the groan of oak or elm, the rustling of a pine. Listen and they will speak to you. Listen carefully and lessons will be taught. Will you take the time to learn?

Trees are patient and can be gentle. They hold great wisdom for they have been around for eons of years. Respect the spirit of the trees and they will respect you and teach you well. Are you ready to listen?

Here is what Queen Jejaia told me about the tree and bush faeries.

Tree faeries have a tendency to be more elfin in attitude and appearance. They, along with their cousins who guard over the bushes, often intermingle with the brownies and the sprites along with other sub-species of elf and faerie.

Many tree spirits are ancient and are considered wise. They have strong fortitudes and are long-lived. Their power and energies are to be respected. You don't want to cross a tree spirit.

Trees work with a variety of energies including fey/elf and other subtle intelligent energies. The tree faeries work in harmony to aid these various other energies and beings.

Most tree faeries work with the animals and birds that nest in the branches of their respective trees and develop colors for the leaves for decoration during the spring and autumn season. They also aid the bark and wood during the summer and winter months.

The faeries of the trees all have their favorite species of tree and much like humans with their favorite sport teams are loyal to their species. Much friendly rivalry may occur among the faeries as each tends to their own type of tree or bush.

Here then are a handful of trees and the faeries that work with them:

Ash – These faeries tend to be on the snobbish side. They are fierce in their loyalty and can be warrior-like in this respect. They are noble and strong beings. The help fight off the ash bore, a destructive insect that feeds off the ash and can kill these fine trees.

Beech – These are fine faeries that tend to be very intelligent and are known to gather histories. They are scholars and are renowned for their kind demeanor and worldly manners. They love to argue politics and are great debaters.

Elm – These faeries are fine artisans and are sensitive souls. They help paint the color of elm leaves during the seasons and play with the squirrels and birds that nest among the elm branches.

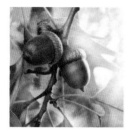 **Oak** – The oak harbors a type of "solider faerie." These faeries are strong both mentally and physically. They help protect other trees nearby and aid in communicative cooperation. They also help paint the leaves, especially in the spring and autumn.

These faeries are boastful when it comes to their acorn harvests, which helps feed both squirrel and feathered friends during winter months. They are also known to be creative and playful; and love to party when their work is done. Loyalty and hardworking are their known attributes.

Maple – Very loving and romantic are the faeries that live among the maple branches. They help with producing the sap that turns into syrup and in the autumn they are known for their beautiful leaf painting. They work with the insects that feast on the maple leaves, to thwart disease and damage to the tree. They are great story tellers and wonderful musicians.

Pine – These faeries are guardians and long-lived. They are also gatherers – meaning they hunt down various food supplies and bring them back to their individual kingdoms. Pine needles are a particular delicacy for the faeries and the pine tree faeries are in charge of farming this food for their citizens. Winter is a favorite time of year for these faeries and they often engage in a variety of cold weather activities, both for work and play.

*Any tree in any backyard may have faeries or
have powerful energies attached to it.*

Chapter Thirteen:
Learning More about the Faeries

Here you'll find a list of books that teach you more about faeries—books which I used to help create this book.

There is a vast world of stories and tales about the faerie world, along with tales of gods, goddesses and beings that rule the elements of air, water, earth and fire. These are tales that you can read and gain a vast amount of knowledge of the legend and lore of the faerie world and the world of nature elementals.

I have listed the tales by title and their origin, along with what they pertain to in the fey world. This list is by no means extensive and only touches on the vast amount of material found in literature. Please also don't forget the vast and wide amount of contemporary material being written, painted and sculpted that deals with the world of faeries.

Here is a brief list, which includes a short story that I wrote several years ago about elves. Most of these books or stories can be found in libraries, in your local bookstore or on-line. I know my short story can still be found in the book which is located on www.Amazon.com.

Tales of Ali Baba – Arabian folk tale (*earth*)

Rumpelstilskin – German folk tale (*earth*)

Snow White and Rose Red – German folktale (*earth*)

Rip Van Winkle – United States folktale (*earth*)

British Tales of Robin Good fellow (*earth*)

A Midnight Summer's Dream by William Shakespeare *(earth)*

The Little Mermaid – Danish folktale or yes, the Disney tale *(water)*

Jason and the Argonauts – Greek tales *(water)*

Odysseus and the Sirens – Greek mythology *(water)*

The Crane and the Turtle – Japanese folktale *(water)*

The Six Swans – German folktale *(water)*

St George and the Dragon – British folktale *(fire)*

Aladdin and His Wonderful Lamp – Middle Eastern folktale *(air)*

"A Soul to be Gained" by Blake Cahoon – found in the book "Elf Magic", edited by Martin H. Greenberg. Published by DAW book and found on Amazon.com. *(earth)*

Chapter Fourteen:
Thank you for coming....

And learning about the world of the faeries. Both Queen Jejaia and I thank you for taking this journey with us—as well as Oscar, King Duke and Prince Stephan.

We've only started to touch upon the world of the faeries and we hope you continue to explore this fascinating world.

I know that this magical world of faeries, while it may seem to be simply fantasy and spun in the minds of faerie tale tellers and childhood dreams, have become very real for me over this last year.

Once you realize something is real, it's hard to deny the truth of what was once deemed only a fantasy and a childhood dream. And that is the beauty of this world –dreams do come true – as long we dreamers can continue to believe that they will.

May all your dreams come true too!

Afterword

This book was started in 2003; as I write these words it is the day after Christmas 2014....and the new year of 2015 is days away. I've done my best to bridge the gap between the time periods of this book's creation.

It's been many a year since I first encountered the faeries in my Oak Park, Illinois bedroom. My journey with spiritual beings of every shape, type and size remains a fascinating one.

This past spring I held true to my word to Oscar and held a faerie workshop. During the presentation they again showed their presence, much to my surprise, when they changed a slide during a meditation. One eyeful student actually saw the faerie culprit!

One skeptic student became a believer!

Remember to respect faeries if chosen to work with them. Indeed, while they are from the angelic realm on a technical level, they indeed are really a different breed of cat, so to speak.

There are many resources beyond what I've presented in this book to find out more about the faerie realm. An internet search should provide you much material.

Just as we were finishing up this latest edition, I learned that King Duke is no longer with us—his son Stephan is now King of the faerie realm I currently live in. He stated however he wanted to keep his father's honor alive and keep my manuscript the way it is. I have done so, out of respect for his wishes.

The faerie people are a wonderful people, whose kindness and consideration towards humans who honor Mother Nature and our Earth are second to none. I invite you to make contact with your local faerie realm.

Remember that your first step is to Believe--and never stop. Only then can you truly experience the wonder and world of faeries, elementals and nature spirits.

Blake Cahoon
Pleasant Prairie, Wisconsin
December 2014

Bibliography

Andrews, Ted. *Enchantment of the Faerie Realm: Communicate with Nature Spirits & Elementals.* St. Paul, MN: Llewellyn Publications, 2001.

Virtue, Ph.D., Doreen. *Healing with the faeries: Messages, Manifestations, and Love from the World of the faeries.* Carlsbad, CA: Hay House Inc., 2001.

Virtue, Ph.D., Doreen. *Earth Angels: A Pocket Guide for Incarnated Angels, Elementals, Starpeople, Walk-Ins, and Wizards.* Carlsbad, CA: Hay House Inc., 2002.

Webster, Richard. *Spirit Guides & Angel Guardians: Contact Your Invisible Helpers.* Woodbury, MN: Llewellyn Publications, 1998.

Picture and Photo Credits

We have done the best of our abilities to ensure all photos and pictures are either in the public domain or we have purchased permission to use. These are their sources and we say thank you for their use:

PDPhoto.org, John Sullivan
Public-domain-photos.com
Public-domain-weekly snaps
Canned Stock Photos
RF123 Stock Photos
Public Domain-Karen'sWhimsy.com
Wikimedia Commons
Other Photos: Blake Cahoon

Notes

Notes

0

About Blake Cahoon

Blake Cahoon is a writer whose belief in subjects spiritual and metaphysical has offered her a life filled with adventure, great love, and magical days.

She is a spiritual person whose support system includes not only God, family, friends, and felines, but also more esoteric beings such as angels and ascended masters.

For many years, her business, The Angelic Path, has been providing people with a means to communicate with our non-physical unseen worlds that provide us with so much wisdom, love and delight. You'll find all of Blake's books for sale on the web site as well as Amazon.com.

The Angelic Path, which you can find at: www.TheAngelicPath.com is her vehicle to teach about a world beyond our own where wishes and dreams can come true.

Blake teaches both locally and on the web, about angels, spirit guides and faeries and the magic and support these loving beings can bring to us all. Sign up on the web site to receive news about the latest classes and events.

In 2013, Blake moved to Wisconsin near Lake Michigan and lives on a prairie reserve. Her adventures with faeries continue, as she is making friends with the faerie kingdom she has found there.

About Twilight Sky Media

Twilight Sky Media is proud to publish books about esoteric subject matter, as well as metaphysical, paranormal and spiritual subjects. They also specialize in self-growth and personal development books, DVDs, CDs and other media.

Connecting with Nature's Angels is one offering of many in the Twilight Sky Media family. They are located in Wisconsin.